Clean Water

A Choral Dialectic
for Unaccompanied SATB Choir

- Secretary Michael

"Clean Water"
Choral Dialectic
by Secretary Michael

ISBN: 978-1-888712-36-0

What is a Choral Dialectic?

A "choral dialectic" is a four-movement choral work (with or without instruments) in which a rational argument about any subject is battled-out musically. There's only one rule: every choral dialectic must use the following four titles for its four movements:

1. "PRINCIPLE"
Each dialectic begins with a statement of some sort. This will be the subject matter for the entire work. Oftentimes the statement is an ideal - an expression of how something might be in a perfect world.

2. "ARGUMENT"
In this movement, the "Principle" begins its journey through the meat grinder. The Argument's job is to pick apart the principle, either supporting it or challenging it.

3. "COUNTERARGUMENT"
In this movement, the "Principle" gets supported or challenged again, but this time from a contrasting perspective. If the previous argument was sweet, this one will probably be sour. If the previous was about abundance, this one will probably be about scarcity.

4. "RESOLUTION"
Now that the "Principle" has been analyzed from different angles, some sort of final understanding will have to emerge. Maybe there will be growth, a new way of being, a new way of living in the world, a new "Principle". Or maybe not.

Machinists Union Press
web: www.machinistsunion.org
email: twimfina@gmail.com

Clean Water

Duration: Less than 12 minutes

Principle

(from the "Clean Water" choral dialectic)

Words and Music: Secretary Michael

$\quad \quad = 100$

A: I be - lieve that we're all much the same, so if some-thing is harm-ful to me then I

A: must use my bo - dy and brain to make sure that o - thers are free. I be -

A: lieve that we're all much the same, so if some-thing is harm-ful to me then I

B: I be-lieve that we're all much the same, so if some-thing is harm-ful to me

A: must use my bo - dy and brain to make sure that o - thers are free. I be -

B: then I must use my bo - dy and brain to make sure that o - thers are free.

Measure 37 (SATB):
I think drink-ing sew - age would be some-thing ve-ry harm-ful to me.

(Alto, additional): I be

Measures 41–44:

Chords: Bb Bb(sus4) Bb · Eb · Dm · Eb · Bb · F7

I be-lieve that we're all much the same, so if some-thing is harm-ful to me
(Alto): lieve that we're all much the same, so if some-thing is harm-ful to me then I

Measures 45–48:

Chords: Bb Bb(sus4) Bb · Eb · Dm · Eb · F7 · Bb

then I must use my bo-dy and brain to make sure that o-thers are free.
(Alto): must use my bo-dy and brain to make sure that o-thers are free.

Argument

(from the "Clean Water" choral dialectic)

Words and Music: Secretary Michael

S: Drip drip drip drip / Drip drip drip drip / Drip drip drip drip

A: Drop drop drop drop / Drop drop drop drop

T: Wa-ter, wa-ter way up high,

S: Drip drip drip drip / Drip drip drip drip / Drip drip drip drip

A: Drop drop drop drop / Drop drop drop drop / Drop drop drop

T: Wait-ing, wait-ing in the sky. When it's time, we hear the drums, the sig-nals flash and down it comes!

7
B♭ Gm E♭ F B♭ Gm
S
YAY! (pitchless shout) It's rain - ing, it's rain - ing with light-ning and thun-der and all of us crea-tures are
A
YAY! (pitchless shout) Rain - ing, rain - ing, light - ning, thun - der. All us crea - tures
T
YAY! (pitchless shout) Rain - ing, rain - ing, light - ning, thun - der. All us crea - tures
B
YAY! (pitchless shout) Rain - ing, rain - ing, light - ning, thun - der. All us crea - tures
11
E♭ F Cm Dm E♭ Dm Cm Dm
S
smil - ing in won- der. The hor-ses are hors- ing, gir - affes are gir - af- fing, the pig-gies are pig-ging and
A
smile in won- der. Hor-ses are hors- ing, gir - affes are gir - af- fing, the pig-gies are pig-ging and
T
smile in won- der. Hor-ses are hors- ing, gir - affes are gir - af- fing, the pig-gies are pig-ging and
B
smile in won- der. Hor-ses are hors- ing, gir - affes are gir - af- fing, the pig-gies are pig-ging and

15

S: e-v'ry-one's laugh-ing. It's rain-ing, it's rain-ing, the woods are all sap-py. The plants and the a-ni-mals

A: e-v'ry-one's laugh-ing. It's rain - ing, rain - ing woods are sap-py.__ Plants and a-ni-mals

T: e-v'ry-one's laugh-ing. It's rain - ing, rain - ing woods are sap-py.__ Plants and a-ni-mals

B: e-v'ry-one's laugh-ing. It's rain - ing, rain - ing woods are sap-py.__ Plants and a-ni-mals

Chords: E♭ F⁷ B♭ Gm E♭ F B♭ Gm

19

S: drink and are hap-py. The goo-ses are goo-sing, the ga-tors are ga-ting, the moo-ses are moo-sing, they're

A: drink, are hap-py.__ Goo ses are goo-sing, the ga-tors are ga-ting, the moo-ses are moo-sing, they're

T: drink, are hap-py.__ Goo ses are goo-sing, the ga-tors are ga-ting, the moo-ses are moo-sing, they're

B: drink, are hap-py.__ Goo ses are goo-sing, the ga-tors are ga-ting, the moo-ses are moo-sing, they're

Chords: E♭ F Cm Dm E♭ Dm Cm Dm

23
E♭ F7 B♭ Gm E♭ E♭m
S
all ce - le - bra - ting: Wa - ter.__ Wa - ter.__ Clean, Safe,
A
all ce - le - bra - ting: Wa- ter.__ Wa- ter. Wa- ter.__ Wa - ter. Clean, Safe,
T
all ce - le- bra - ting: Wa- ter. Wa- ter.__ Wa- ter. Wa- ter.__ Clean, Safe,
B
all ce - le- bra - ting: Wa- ter. Wa- ter.__ Wa- ter. Wa- ter.__ Clean, Safe,
27
B♭ B♭ Gm
S
Wa - ter. Drip drip drip drip Drip drip drip drip Drip drip drip drip
A
Wa - ter. Drop drop drop drop Drop drop drop drop
T
Wa - ter. Wa- ter, wa-ter trick-ling down,
B
Wa - ter.

Drip drip drip drip Drip drip drip drip Drip drip drip drip

Drop drop drop drop Drop drop drop drop Drop drop drop

Lit-tle streams a-long the ground. In-to brooks from near and far and fill-ing up our re-ser-voir.

YAY! (pitchless shout) It's wa-ter! It's wa-ter! It's roll-ing and flow-ing, and flow-ers all o-ver are

YAY! (pitchless shout) Wa-ter! Wa-ter! Roll-ing, flow-ing. Flow-ers all are

YAY! (pitchless shout) Wa-ter! Wa-ter! Roll-ing, flow-ing. Flow-ers all are

YAY! (pitchless shout) Wa-ter! Wa-ter! Roll-ing, flow-ing. Flow-ers all are

38 — Eb | F | Cm | Dm | Eb | Dm | Cm | Dm

S: bloom-ing and grow-ing. The pumps are all pump-ing, the fish are all jump-ing, the whales are all spout-ing, the

A: bloom - ing, grow- ing.__ Pumps are all pump-ing, the fish are all jump-ing, the whales are all spout-ing, the

T: bloom - ing, grow- ing.__ Pumps are all pump-ing, the fish are all jump-ing, the whales are all spout-ing, the

B: bloom - ing, grow- ing.__ Pumps are all pump-ing, the fish are all jump-ing, the whales are all spout-ing, the

42 — Eb | F⁷ | Bb | Gm | Eb | F | Bb | Gm

S: trout are all shout-ing. It's wa - ter! It's wa-ter! Cas - ca-ding and crash-ing, so life can go on and on

A: trout are all shout-ing. It's wa - ter! Wa-ter! Cas-ca - ding, crash- ing.__ Life can go on

T: trout are all shout-ing. It's wa - ter! Wa-ter! Cas - ca - ding, crash- ing.__ Life can go on

B: trout are all shout-ing. It's wa - ter! Wa-ter! Cas-ca - ding, crash- ing.__ Life can go on

46
E♭ F Cm Dm E♭ Dm Cm Dm
S
splish ing and splash- ing. The king-fish are bow- ing, the cat fish me-ow ing, there'sdrink-ing and drank-ing with
A
splish - ing, splash- ing.__ King-fish are bow- ing, the cat fish me-ow ing, there'sdrink-ing and drank-ing with
T
splish - ing, splash- ing.__ King-fish are bow- ing, the cat fish me-ow ing, there'sdrink-ing and drank-ing with
B
splish - ing, splash- ing.__ King-fish are bow- ing, the cat fish me-ow ing, there'sdrink-ing and drank-ing with
50
E♭ F7 B♭ Gm E♭ E♭m B♭
S
all the world thank- ing: Wa - ter.__ Wa - ter.__ Clean, Safe, Wa- ter.
A
all the world thank - ing: Wa- ter.__ Wa- ter. Wa- ter.__ Wa- ter.Clean, Safe, Wa- ter.
T
all the world thank- ing: Wa- ter. Wa-ter._ Wa- ter. Wa-ter._ Clean, Safe, Wa- ter.
B
all the world thank - ing: Wa- ter. Wa-ter._ Wa- ter. Wa-ter._ Clean, Safe, Wa- ter.

Counterargument

(from the "Clean Water" choral dialectic)

Words and Music: Secretary Michael

S: There are some words that don't de-serve a me-lo-dy,

A: don't de-serve a me-lo-dy,

S: that don't de-serve a har-mo-ny, but they are words that we must hear, we must

A: don't de-serve a har-mo-ny, but they are words that we must hear, we must

S: hear, they are words that we must hear.

A: hear, they are words that we must hear.

T: Words like "ty-phoid". Words like

B: Ty-phoid.

15

T: "cho - le - ra". The words that mil - lions fear. These are the

B: Cho - le - ra. Fear. These are the

18

T: words that we must hear.

B: words that we must hear.

22 Sal - mo - nel - la, Shi - gel - lo - sis, Fe - cal - Or - al Di - ag - no - sis.

B:

(Spoken in a forceful and punctuated manner)

24 Cryp - to, Lep - to, En - ter - i - tis, Di - ar - rhe - a, He - pa - ti - tis.

B:

26

S: Wa - ter

A: Dir - ty

B: Sal - mo - nel - la, Shi - gel - lo - sis, Fe - cal - Or - al Di - ag - no - sis.

34

S: Thirs - ty, thirs - ty, thirs - ty, thirs - ty. Wa - - ter

A: Dir - - ty Thirs - ty, thirs - ty, thirs - ty, thirs - ty.

T: Dir - - ty, dir - ty wa - - ter.

B: *Sal-mo-nel-la, Shi-gel-lo-sis, Fe-cal Or-al Di-ag-no-sis. Cryp-to, Lep-to, En-ter-i-tis, Di-ar-rhe-a, He-pa-ti-tis.*

36

S: Thirs - ty, thirs - ty, thirs - ty, thirs - ty. Wa - - ter

A: Dir - - ty Thirs - ty, thirs - ty, thirs - ty, thirs - ty.

T: Dir - - ty, dir - ty wa - - ter.

B: *Sal-mo-nel-la, Shi-gel-lo-sis, Fe-cal Or-al Di-ag-no-sis. Cryp-to, Lep-to, En-ter-i-tis, Di-ar-rhe-a, He-pa-ti-tis.*

Measure 38:

S1: Thirs - ty, thirs - ty,

S2: Thirs - ty, thirs - ty, thirs - ty, thirs - ty. Wa - - ter

A: Dir - - ty Thirs - ty, thirs - ty, thirs - ty, thirs - ty.

T: Dir - - ty, dir - ty wa - - ter.

B: Sal-mo-nel-la, Shi-gel-lo-sis, Fe-cal Or-al Di-ag-no-sis. Cryp-to, Lep-to, En-ter-i-tis, Di-ar-rhe-a, He-pa-ti-tis.

Measure 40:

S1: thirs - - ty, thirs - - ty.

S2: Thirs - ty, thirs - ty, thirs - ty, thirs - ty. Wa - - ter

A: Dir - - ty Thirs - ty, thirs - ty, thirs - ty, thirs - ty.

T: Dir - - ty, dir - ty wa - - ter.

B: Sal-mo-nel-la, Shi-gel-lo-sis, Fe-cal Or-al Di-ag-no-sis. Cryp-to, Lep-to, En-ter-i-tis, Di-ar-rhe-a, He-pa-ti-tis.

Forceful and Punctuated:

42

S, A, T, B: Sal - mo - nel - la, Shi - gel - lo - sis, Fe - cal - Or - al Di - ag - no - sis.

44

S, A, T, B: Cryp - to, Lep - to, En - ter - i - tis, Di - ar - rhe - a, He - pa - ti - tis.

Rather softly after a settling pause:

46

S: There are some words that don't de - serve a me - lo - dy,

A: don't de - serve a me - lo - dy,

50

S: that don't de-serve a har-mo-ny, but they are words that we must

A: don't de-serve a har-mo-ny, but they are words that we must

54

S: hear, we must hear, they are words that we must hear.

A: hear, we must hear, they are words that we must hear.

GLOSSARY OF WATERBORNE DISEASES:

Typhoid: Typhoid Fever (up to 104 degrees!) is caused by the Salmonella bacterium passed on from the feces of infected people. Some people (like Typhoid Mary) show no symptoms but can still infect others. Only humans are effected.

Cholera: Cholera is an infection of the small intestine caused by the Vibrio bacterium passed on from the feces of infected people. Cholera causes severe diarrhea. Only humans are effected.

Salmonella: a rod-shaped bacterium; one type (Salmonella typhi) causes typhoid fever, other types cause food poisoning.

Shigellosis: Shigellosis is a disease caused by the Shigella bacterium passed on from the feces of infected people. It causes severe dysentery (bloody diarrhea).

Fecal-Oral: Waterborne diseases are largely the result from feces (fecal) contamination of the water which then enters the mouth (oral).

Crypto: Cryptosporidiosis is a disease caused by the potozoan parasite Cryptosporidium. It infects the intestines. It is spread when it forms dormant cysts which are passed on through the feces to contaminate water.

Lepto: Leptospirosis is caused by the corskscrew-shaped bacterium Leptospira. It is spread from the urine of infected animals. Among its possible symptoms, a person can turn yellow in color.

Enteriris: a medical term that refers to inflammation of the small intestine (a common result of waterborne diseases).

Diarrhea: the official definition is "having at least 3 loose or liquid bowel movements in one day". Diarrhea is a common symptom of waterborne diseases. (Maybe the pathogens cause frequent bowel movements so that they can spread to more and more people). Diarrhea can lead to dehydration and death. (Over a million people - mostly children - die from diarrhea every year).

Hepatitis: inflamation of the liver; two of the viruses that cuase hepatitis (Hepatitis A and Hepatitis E) can be spread through contaminated water;

There are plenty of additional waterborne disease words that I wasn't clever enough to fit into the meter and rhyme scheme. Words such as: Schistosomiasis (snail fever), Giardiasis (beaver fever), Dracunculiasis (Guinea worm disease), Taeniasis (tapeworm disease), Campylobacteriosis...

Learning about these fecal-oral diseases and parasites leads us to be more conscientious about washing our hands before eating (to protect ourselves) and washing our hands after using the restroom (to protect others). It also leads us to help those whose water does not serve as the prevention of disease but rather as the source of disease.

* Source of Waterborne Disease information: Wikipedia

Resolution

(from the "Clean Water" choral dialectic)

Words and Music: Secretary Michael

I be-lieve that we're all much the same, so if some-thing is harm-ful to me, then I

must use my bo-dy and brain to make sure that o-thers are free. I be-

I be-lieve that we're all much the same, so if some-thing is harm-ful to me,

lieve that we're all much the same, so if some-thing is harm-ful to me then I

then I must use my bo-dy and brain to make sure that o-thers are free. And

must use my bo-dy and brain to make sure that o-thers are free.

17

A: I think drink-ing sew - age would be some-thing harm-ful to me. And

B: And

21

A: I think drink-ing sew - age would be some-thing harm-ful to me. And

B: I think drink-ing sew - age would be some-thing harm-ful to me. And

25

S: And

A: I think drink-ing sew - age would be some-thing harm-ful to me. And

T: Sal-mo-nel-la, Shi-gel-lo-sis, Fe-cal-Or-al Di-ag-no-sis. Cryp-to, Lep-to, En - ter-i - tis, Di-ar-rhe-a, He-pa-ti-tis.

B: I think drink-ing sew - age would be some-thing harm-ful to me. And

29
S
I think drink - ing sew - age would be some-thing ve-ry harm-ful to me.___ So
A
I think drink - ing sew - age would be some-thing ve-ry harm-ful to me.___ So
T
Sal-mo-nel-la, Shi-gel-lo-sis, Fe-cal-Or-al Di-ag-no-sis. some-thing ve-ry harm-ful to me.___ So
B
I think drink - ing sew - age would be some-thing ve-ry harm-ful to me.___ So

33
A7
Dm
S
come and join us, let's get this done, let's bring clean wa-ter to e - v'ry-one.__ We've
div.
A
come and join, let's get this done. Let's bring clean wa - ter e - v'ry - one. We've
T
come and join, let's get this done. Let's bring clean wa - ter e - v'ry - one. We've
B
come and join, let's get this done. Let's bring clean wa - ter e - v'ry - one. We've

37
G7
Gm7
C7
S
talked and talked and talked it through. But now the talk-ing has to stop, it's time to go and
A
div.
talked and talked and talked it through. But now the talk-ing has to stop, it's time to go and
T
talked and talked and talked it through. But now the talk-ing has to stop, it's time to go and
B
talked and talked and talked it through. But now the talk-ing has to stop, it's time to go and
41
F F(sus4) F
B♭
Am
B♭
F
S
do. I be-lieve that we're all much the same, so if some-thing is harm-ful to
A
do. I be - lieve that we're all much the same, so if some-thing is harm-ful to
T
do. I be-lieve that we're all much the same, so if some-thing is harm-ful to
B
do. I be-lieve that we're all much the same, so if some-thing is harm-ful to

Measure 45:
me — then I must use my bo-dy and brain to make sure that o-thers are free. We

Measure 50:
have the peo-ple, we have the dreams, we have the know-ledge, we have the means. So

let's con - ti - nue   what we've be - gun,___   let's push and push and push and push un-

let's con - ti - nue   we've be - gun, let's   push and push and push and push un -

let's con - ti - nue   we've be - gun, let's   push and push and push and push un -

let's con - ti - nue   we've be - gun, let's   push and push and push and push un -

til we get this done! Let's   push and push and push and push un - til we get this done!   Clean

til we get this done! Let's   push and push and push and push un - til we get this done!   Clean

til we get this done! Let's   push and push and push and push un - til we get this done!   Clean

til we get this done! Let's   push and push and push and push un - til we get this done!   Clean

Lyrics, measure 60:
Wa - ter! Wa - ter! Fresh and de - li - cious for all of the peo - ple, the plants and the fish - es. The

Wa - ter! Wa - ter! Fresh, de - li - cious.__ All the peo - ple, plants and fish - es. The

Lyrics, measure 64:
fau - cets are flow - ing, the flow - ers are grow - ing, there's so much e - la - tion and such ce - le - bra - tion for

68

S: wa - ter, wa - ter, all that we're wish-ing. The kids__ are laugh ing and splash-ing and splish-ing. With

A: Wa - ter! Wa - ter! All we're wish - ing.__ Kids are laugh - ing, splash - ing splish-ing. With

T: Wa - ter! Wa - ter! All we're wish-ing.__ Kids are laugh - ing, splash - ing, splish-ing. With

B: Wa - ter! Wa - ter! All we're wish-ing.__ Kids are laugh - ing, splash - ing, splish-ing. With

72

S: no-thing for fear-ing, the peo ple are cheer-ing. Our cups are all clink-ing and e - v'ry-one's drink - ing

A: no-thing for fear-ing, the peo ple are cheer-ing. Our cups are all clink-ing and e - v'ry-one's drink - ing

T: no-thing for fear-ing, the peo ple are cheer-ing. Our cups are all clink-ing and e - v'ry-one's drink - ing

B: no-thing for fear-ing, the peo ple are cheer-ing. Our cups are all clink-ing and e - v'ry-one's drink - ing

Some clean water projects that might be worth contributing to:

The Water Project (thewaterproject.org)
Charity: Water (charitywater.org)
Water.org (water.org)
The World Bank (worldbank.org)
Shoeman Water Projects (shoemanwater.org)
African Water Facility (africanwaterfacility.org)
Water Wells For Africa (waterwellsforafrica.org)
Africa Heartwood Project (africaheartwoodproject.org)
World Vision (worldvision.org)
Water Aid (wateraid.org)
Water for Life (un.org)

But whichever organization you choose, please first check its transparency and effectiveness:

Charity Navigator (charitynavigator.org)
Charity Check (charitycheck101.org)
Charity Choices (charitychoices.com)

Recent Works by Secretary Michael

Jo Puma - Wild Choir Music
Collection of 36 traditional "Sacred Harp" arrangements with new secular lyrics for our diverse society. This collection has removed the 3 barriers that have kept this music out of our schools: inappropriate lyrics, poor shape-note legibility, and nonstandard use of standard solfege names. Now we all have a chance to experience this exciting early American music. (Book available; check for free download: www.machinistsunion.org/works. html)

Secular Hymnal
Collection of 144 favorite hymn tunes from around the world. The hymn tunes have been re-notated and given thoughtful egalitarian lyrics that promote peace. Many public schools use them for choral sight-reading practice. Available in both unison/guitar and SATB choir editions. Now we all have a chance to share in these musical treasures. (Books available; check for free download: www.machinistsunion.org/works.html)

Twimfina
A peace-themed musical play for singing groups of all ages. The story is about a young woman named "Twimfina" (an acronym for "The World Is My Family, I'm Not Afraid") who runs off to a hostile country. It is scored for voice and piano. The play is divided into 21 segments, many of which can stand alone. This allows an acting group to perform individual segments instead of the entire 2.5 hour play. (Book available; check for free download: www.machinistsunion.org/works.html)

Choral Dialectics
A "choral dialectic" is a 4-movement choral work (with or without instruments) in which a rational argument is battled-out musically. There's only one rule: every choral dialectic must use the following four titles for its four movements: "Principle" - "Argument" - "Counterargument" - "Resolution"
Secretary Michael has begun working on a series of 6 choral dialectics, some of which are available now; the rest will become available as they are completed in future years. (Books available; check for free downloads: www. machinistsunion.org/works.html)

Aren't We the Lucky Ones
A book-length story about a group of college science students who share an understanding that people don't truly have a free will. There are no "good people" or "bad people", just lucky and unlucky ones. This insight carries with it the responsibility to protect the "unlucky" from the wrath of the "lucky". The students form a community in order to live out their ideals. (Book available - both paperback and digital).

Joy of Piggyback Songs
Dozens of fun, short choral works in which more than one melody is sung at the same time. Book (and free internet download) will become available after it is completed.

"Please help create public choirs that are free from religious and nationalistic content so that all singers feel welcome."

- Secretary Michael

www.ingramcontent.com/pod-product-compliance
Lightning Source LLC
Chambersburg PA
CBHW080536030426
42337CB00023B/4763